CONTENTS

ONCE I WAS A CARDBOARD BOX... BUT NOW I'M A BOOK ABOUT POLAR BEARS!

I started my life as a cardboard box, but now I've been turned into a book!

Books are usually made from three things:

PAPER for books is usually made from wood. Old comics, newspapers, magazines, and other paper products are turned into new paper. This is called *recycled* paper. It is often more expensive than brand new paper, but it saves trees from being cut down and saves energy.

BOARD is used to make the stiff cover of a book. It is often made from recycled paper and cardboard and is called *greyboard*.

PLASTIC The shiny cover of most books is made from very thin plastic called *laminate*. It is kind of like plastic wrap.

This book is made only of recycled paper and board. We didn't use any plastic on the cover, which is why it isn't shiny.

So, what is this book about? **POLAR BEARS!** (And also about boxes!) The polar bear is in danger of extinction. This book tells you all about polar bears and how you can help them survive. The more we help care for our environment, the more chance the polar bear and other endangered animals have of surviving.

Where Polar Bears Live

Polar bears live near the North Pole. Only five countries in the world have polar bears. They are:

- **Russia**
- **Greenland**
- **U.S. (but only in Alaska)**
- **Canada**
- **Norway**

Hello, I live near the North Pole.

CANADA

ALASKA

4

Survival

Polar bears belong to the same family as other bears, but they have adapted to living on the Arctic ice.

FRONT PAWS are like paddles for swimming. They have **SMALL BUMPS** called *papillae* (puh-pil-ee) to stop their feet from slipping on the ice.

LITTLE EARS so the bears don't lose much heat

GOOD SENSE OF SMELL to sniff out prey. Polar bears can smell a seal up to a mile away!

LONG NECK compared to other bears, to keep head above water when swimming.

BIG PAWS for walking on snow and ice, and **STRONG CLAWS** for catching prey.

BEAR FACT
Polar bears are the biggest predators on land, almost twice as big as lions and tigers.

The factory that made me sold me to another factory that makes toys.

100 little boxes of toy tractors were packed inside me.

BACK PAWS like rudders to steer.

SHORT TAIL to help prevent heat loss.

Keeping Warm

It's difficult to imagine how cold it is at the North Pole. In winter, temperatures drop to -50°F (-45°C), which is twice as cold as the freezers in supermarkets.

BEAR FACT

Polar bears have a layer of fat, called *blubber*, about as thick as your leg.

I was put in a big container with lots of other boxes and sent by sea to the U.S.

Luckily, polar bears have two layers of fur to keep them warm. Did you know that polar bears aren't actually white? Their fur is a yellowish color, but it looks white because the hair reflects light from the bright snow.

Each hair is a hollow tube, like a drinking straw. This helps the bears dry off quickly after they've been swimming.

Then I was sent to a toyshop.

Baby Bears

Polar bears usually have two babies (or cubs) each year. When the mother is pregnant, she digs a den, called a *maternity* den, in the snow to keep the babies safe and warm.

BEAR FACT

The female bear has to gain at least 441 lbs. (200 kg) when she is pregnant—that's the weight of 50 cats!

The cubs are born in November or December. A newborn polar bear is about the size of a loaf of bread. The cubs have no teeth. They are blind and have short fur.

The mother bear stays with her babies in the maternity den until March or April. She does not eat or drink during the time she is in the den. Imagine that!

Little Bears

Baby polar bears live in the den for the first few months of their lives. Their mother keeps them warm. She feeds them her milk that smells like seals or fish. They grow very quickly.

BEAR FACT

Polar bears sleep for 7-8 hours at a time, like humans. They also enjoy taking naps!

I was put in a big container and spent weeks with lots of other squashed boxes.

After about four months, the cubs are big enough to leave the den. They play outside, but they return to their mother for milk.

A big truck came and took us to a recycling factory.

Polar Bear Facts

You've learned a lot of interesting things about polar bears by now, but here are some more facts for you to get your paws on...

- Polar bears have 42 teeth.

- They can gallop as fast as a horse over short distances. They are so well-padded that they can overheat.

- When the ice is very thin, they crawl or slide on their bellies so the ice won't crack.

- Scientists know the age of a polar bear by examining a slice of tooth and counting the layers—just like trees!

- Each paw measures up to 1 ft. (31cm) across, which is bigger than a dinner plate.

- Polar bears keep themselves very clean.

- Depending on the season or where they live, polar bears change color.

The factory dumped us on a conveyor belt.

We went into a big machine that crunched us into little pieces.

15

Leaving Home

The baby bears get stronger and learn how to do things to help them survive as adults.

Their mothers teach them everything they need to know about living in the Arctic.

When the bears are about two years old, they are big enough to leave their mothers and hunt on their own.

The little pieces got mixed with water and we were made into a squishy mess called *pulp*.

The pulp went into another machine and we got made into brown paper.

BEAR FACT
Polar bears are happy to share their food as long as they have enough to survive.

Hunting

Polar bears travel to the ocean to catch food. The bears can swim a long way. They have been found as far as 60 mi. (100 km) from land! That's about 4,000 lengths of a normal swimming pool.

Polar bears like to eat seals most of all. They hunt by sitting beside a seal's breathing hole in the ice. When the seal pops up to get air, the bear pounces and grabs the seal with its huge claws or teeth.

The brown paper was made into a huge roll, bigger than a person.

I think I was somewhere in the middle!

BEAR FACT
A polar bear's stomach can hold about 15–20 percent of its body weight.

Polar Bears and Native People

In the past, polar bears were hunted by the native people of the Arctic. The meat was eaten and the fur was used for clothing. Nothing would be wasted because food was very hard to find.

Even though the native people hunted polar bears, they also worshipped them. Historians have found cave paintings of polar bears more than 1,500 years old!

The native people may have learned some important survival lessons from the polar bear. Some people now think that the igloo was an imitation of the polar bear's maternity den!

Our roll of brown paper was sent to a factory in China on a big ship.

The roll was put in a huge machine and we were cut into big sheets.

Global Warming

Polar bears only live in very cold places—on ice and in the icy water surrounding it. Sadly, Earth is getting warmer because of pollution. This is called *global warming.*

As the earth gets warmer, the ice in the coldest parts of the world slowly melts. This means the polar bears' home is getting smaller and they have fewer places to hunt for food.

BEAR FACT
In 2008, the polar bear was officially declared an endangered species.

Some scientists think that if the ice continues to melt, many of the world's polar bears will disappear. Other scientists think that the polar bears will adapt by finding food in different places. They might start to eat salmon like grizzly bears do.

The recycled paper was sent to a printing factory that makes books.

I was made into a book about polar bears!

What might happen to me next?

What can YOU do?

Recycling means making old products into new products. This uses much less energy than making things all over again and helps to protect the environment. When trash is thrown away, it gets buried in the ground at something called a *landfill*. This is bad for the environment!

🐾 Recycle as much garbage as you can at home—the easiest things to recycle are newspapers, plastic, aluminum cans, and glass.

🐾 If you have a garden, create compost from the garden waste. The compost makes the soil perfect for plants.

RECYCLING ISN'T JUST ABOUT GARBAGE!

🐾 Why not swap books, toys, and games with friends when you have finished using them? Don't forget to ask your parents first!

🐾 Take cloth bags with you instead of getting plastic bags.

Making small changes will make a big difference. Saving energy helps slow down climate change and saves the polar bear.

Try to recycle as much as you can. It helps conserve the world's resources and protects natural habitats for the future.

WRITTEN by Anton Poitier
ILLUSTRATED by Melvyn Evans
DESIGNED by Clare Barber
EDITED by Georgia Barrington

PHOTO CREDITS
Front Cover © NHPA / photoshot · p.2 © Eric Baccega / naturepl.com
p.4 © iStockphoto · p.5 © iStockphoto · p.6/7 © NHPA/photoshot
p.8 © NHPA/ photoshot · p.12/13 © Wayne R. Bilenduke (The Image Bank) /
Getty Images. · p. 14/15 © Terry Andrewartha / naturepl.com
p. 16 © SeaPics.com · p.18/19 © SeaPics.com · p. 21 © Eric Baccega /
naturepl.com · p.22/23 © Kennan Ward / CORBIS · Back Cover ©
T. Davis/W. Bilenduke (Stone) / Getty Images

© 2009 Tony Potter Publishing Ltd, RH17 5PA
First Published in the United Kingdom by Tony Potter Publishing Ltd
RH17 5PA · www.tonypotter.com

First published in the United Kingdom by Potter Books, an imprint
of Tony Potter Publishing Ltd.

Printed in PRC

This edition published for Scholastic Inc., 557 Broadway,
New York, NY 10012

Scholastic and Associated Logos are trademarks and/or
registered trademarks of Scholastic Inc.

Distributed by: Scholastic Canada Ltd.; Markham, Ontario
ISBN-10: 1-906-72615-9
ISBN-13: 978-1-906-72615-7